A WII
REMEM

**Events recalling the winter of 1962/63
and its effect on the railways of Dartmoor**

by Robert E. Trevelyan

**ARK PUBLICATIONS
(RAILWAYS)**

First published in 1998 by ARK PUBLICATIONS (RAILWAYS), an imprint of
FOREST PUBLISHING, Woodstock, Liverton, Newton Abbot, Devon TQ12 6JJ

British Library Cataloguing in Publication Data
A catalogue record for this book is available from the British Library
ISBN 1-873029-08-X

A wintery scene at Bickleigh Station on the morning of
30th December 1962 – 0–6–0 PT No. 6400 is frozen to
the rails and adorned with icicles formed from melting
snow (before the fire was dropped some hours earlier).

R. E. Taylor

ARK PUBLICATIONS (RAILWAYS)
Editorial, layout and design by:
Mike Lang

Typeset by:
Carnaby Typesetting, Torquay, Devon TQ1 1EG

Printed and bound in Great Britain by:
R. Mann, Newton Abbot, Devon

Cover photographs:

Front – The 12.45pm Plymouth to Tavistock South train, with 0–6–0 PT No. 6400
in charge, at Marsh Mills on 29th December 1962. Because this was
officially the last day of operations on the branch, the locomotive has had
a wreath placed on its smokebox by members of the Plymouth Railway
Circle.

Eric R. Shepherd

Back – An all too common sight on the Southern Region main line between
Okehampton and Tavistock during the winter blizzards of 1962/63. Here,
workmen struggle in their efforts to free 'N' class 2–6–0 No. 31838 which
had been overwhelmed by the snow near Bridestowe on 9th January 1963.
Western Morning News (Courtesy of Anthony R. Kingdom)

CONTENTS

ACKNOWLEDGEMENTS

My thanks are due to the many people who inspired and assisted me both before and during the preparation of this book. Particular thanks are due to:–

Mr John Watts (a former railway employee), who had first told me of his involvement in the events of the winter of 1962/63 as long ago as 1965 and who, during the decidedly wintery weather of February 1996 (which rekindled memories of what he had said and prompted a telephone call), provided me with further information and the inspiration to proceed with this book.

Mr David St. John Thomas for kindly allowing me to use extracts from newspaper articles – previously written by him whilst snowed-in at his home in Cornwood!

Mr Steve Derek (a former member of the staff at Exeter Central Control during 1962/63) for not only providing many previously unpublished photographs but also for offering much encouragement and valuable assistance in tracing various sources of reference and the whereabouts of other photographs.

Mr Peter Gray, the well-known local railway photographer, for also supplying previously unpublished photographs and, in particular, for those taken on 29th December 1962 – the 'last day' trains on the Plymouth, Tavistock & Launceston line.

Mr Robert Zaple for so skilfully originating the two maps that accompany the text.

The staff of the *Express & Echo*, Exeter; the Railway Studies Library, Newton Abbot; the Reference & Information Library, Exeter; the Westcountry Studies Library, Exeter; the *Western Morning News*, Plymouth.

Last, but not least, Mr John Kirton, Mr Dawson Piper (St. Loye's College) and Mr Derek Marsh for providing assistance during the completion of the manuscript, and Mr Eric Beard, Mr Tony Coysh (Abbot Photography) and Mr John Cheesman for assisting with the preparation of the photographs, prior to presentation to the publishers.

(Photographs are acknowledged individually in most instances)

INTRODUCTION

Winter is no respecter of persons, country or transport systems, neither will it always respond to predictions or weather forecasters. In the county of Devon this latter aspect is no more apparent than on Dartmoor, which rises to over 2,000 feet above sea-level and where the variability of the climate is such that heavy mist can gather to blanket its tors, or rain (or snow) descend heavily, out of a seemingly threatless sky.

During the winter of 1947, for example, cold easterly winds were forecast, accompanied by snow, but the intensity of the wind and snow and their combined effect was most certainly not: the ensuing blizzards that swept Dartmoor, and the country as a whole, resulted in it being remembered as one of the worst winters on record.

Because such winters are, thankfully, few and far between in this country, equipment and preparations tend to be rather basic; consequently, we usually get 'caught out'. The media, however, invariably respond by having a field day, with 'experts' declaring that it shouldn't be so. Yet, at the same time, only scant attention is paid to the dedication and professionalism that rises to the surface in those who have to deal with, and work in, such conditions.

It is to this latter group of people that this book is dedicated and to those in particular who were involved in the incidents, during the winter of 1962/63, that affected two railway lines, whose routes traversed parts of northern and western Dartmoor. One of these was the Plymouth, Tavistock & Launceston branch line which, prior to the events that were about to unfold, was scheduled for closure on 29th December 1962 in response to the 'Beeching Axe', while the other was the main line from Exeter to Plymouth and North Cornwall via Okehampton, which was about to be transferred from the Southern Region to its arch rival – the Western Region.

Interestingly enough, resistance to these changes was to come from an unexpected direction and make local headlines during the early months of 1963. The old year had been expected to go out quietly with a cold easterly wind and the odd flurry of snow, but that was not the case at all. Instead, in circumstances similar to those of 1947, intensely cold easterly winds and heavy snow produced widespread blizzards...

Robert E. Trevelyan
Newton Abbot
January 1998

CHAPTER 1

The Line That Wouldn't Die

The branch line running from Plymouth to Tavistock and Launceston left the main Paddington to Penzance line at Tavistock Junction. It then passed through Marsh Mills Station and, on a rising gradient, headed northwards towards Plym Bridge Platform and the beautiful, heavily wooded Plym valley, where it proceeded to cross the river and two of its tributaries by means of three long viaducts before reaching Bickleigh Station. From there, still in a northerly direction, the line soon passed over a fourth viaduct (over yet another tributary of the Plym) and carried on past Shaugh Bridge Platform, just prior to plunging into the darkness of Shaugh tunnel. Emerging from the tunnel, with the River Plym now having veered away to the east and the River Meavy becoming its new companion for a while, the line changed to a more north-westerly direction as it continued towards Clearbrook Halt and Yelverton beyond.

Besides being the first major station along the branch, Yelverton had, for many years, served as the junction for the $10^{1}/_{2}$-mile long Princetown branch. Closed in March 1956, this had been the only passenger line built into the heart of the moor and one that, during the winter of 1962/63, was to be sorely missed by the local populace as roads in the area became impassable.

Immediately upon leaving Yelverton, the line plunged into another tunnel (Yelverton tunnel – 641 yards long) and re-emerged to continue the short distance to the next station – Horrabridge. From there, it was carried across the lower reaches of the Walkham valley by means of two more long viaducts, and then, after passing through Grenofen tunnel, Whitchurch Down Platform was reached, closely followed by the next major station. This was Tavistock South, the terminus for 'local' trains from Plymouth.

Beyond Tavistock, the line continued for a further 19 miles, passing, en route, Mary Tavy and Blackdown Halt (formerly a station), Lydford Station (shared with the Southern Region), Liddaton Halt, Coryton Halt (formerly a station), and Lifton Station (with the 'Ambrosia' milk factory alongside) before terminating at Launceston Station (shared, since 1952, with the Southern Region).

Saturday 29th December 1962

The last official day of operations dawned overcast and with a biting easterly wind already blowing fresh overnight snow into small drifts. Nevertheless, the morning trains ran more or less in accordance with the timetable, and many of the people who were using them were doing so as they had always done, it being their normal mode of transport. Gradually, though, with the weather deteriorating and snow beginning to block some of the surrounding roads and lanes, more and more people started joining

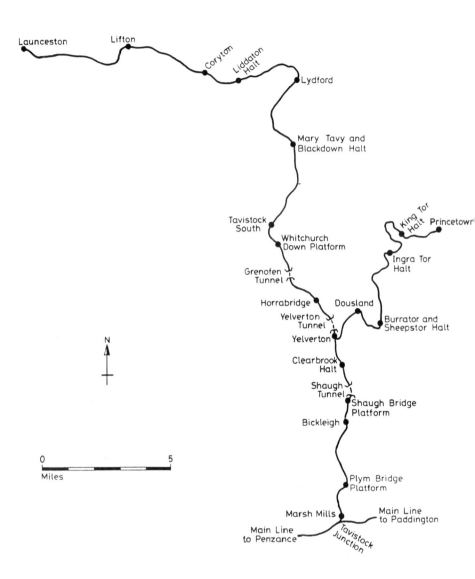

The Plymouth, Tavistock and Launceston Line
(including the Princetown Branch)

The 10.15am Launceston to Plymouth train, hauled by 2–6–2T No. 5569 (complete with wreath above its right-hand buffer), takes a rest at Lydford Station and offers a connection with the 10.02am Plymouth to Waterloo train, which is waiting on the Southern Region platform behind the camera. Although the blizzard was not yet at full strength, this exposed location is quite clearly already suffering from the effect of the deteriorating conditions (29.12.62).

S.P. Derek

the trains, which were being strengthened by additional coaches in order to accommodate numerous railway enthusiasts wishing to make a last trip over the branch.

The first hint of serious problems came when the 12.40pm Launceston to Plymouth train, hauled by small 'Prairie' tank No. 5564, arrived at Lydford – the station, exposed to the wind and swirling snow, was becoming engulfed by the developing drifts! Moreover, it was much the same scenario for the remainder of the journey, with people anxiously waiting on station platforms in conditions that were clearly not going to improve. In spite of this, however, the train completed its journey without too much delay, as did others during the course of the afternoon. These included the 4.30pm Tavistock South to Plymouth, with pannier tank No. 6430 at its head, which just about managed to get through notwithstanding its heavy load in far from ideal conditions.

By now the blizzard was at full strength and causing trouble everywhere. Furthermore, with the temperature dropping to below zero, points became blocked, steam condensed and froze (causing the locking and seizing of joints, pipes and levers) and brake rigging became encrusted with snow. For the passengers, meanwhile, there was the added misery of heating systems failing, their pipes becoming frozen as well.

Out in the countryside near Brentor. 2–6–2T No. 5564, with the 10.40am Plymouth to Launceston train, being overtaken by 'BB' class 4–6–2 No. 34056 *Croydon* on its journey from Plymouth to Brighton (29.12.62).

Peter W. Gray

Another view of the 10.40am Plymouth to Launceston train as it speeds past the 'back door' of Brentor Station, on the route of the Southern Region main line between Okehampton and Plymouth (29.12.62).

S. P. Derek

Because of the worsening conditions, the last two scheduled trains (the 8.40pm Plymouth to Launceston and the 8.35pm Launceston to Plymouth) had both to be cancelled. Consequently, the last train to leave Plymouth for Launceston turned out to be the 6.20pm, hauled by No. 5568. However, due to delays on the main line, this train was some 70 minutes late in leaving and, even then, progressed only as far as Tavistock Junction before a much longer delay ensued – the 5.40pm train from Launceston (running 'wrong line' and very late because of frozen points at Marsh Mills) had yet to clear the section!

Eventually, after strenuous efforts made by the staff at Marsh Mills and Tavistock Junction to clear the 'down' line, the Plymouth-bound train was able to continue its journey, ultimately arriving at its destination at 10.25pm. In the meantime, with the 'down' line clear once more, the Launceston-bound train was finally on the move and slowly making its way up the Plym valley towards Bickleigh, this in spite of one of its four modern Mk 1 coaches having developed brake problems as a result of the extreme conditions.

At Bickleigh the situation was different to that at Marsh Mills inasmuch that the station staff had succeeded in clearing the points at each end of the passing loop, thereby enabling the Launceston-bound train to continue largely unhindered. At the same time, however, the last train out of Tavistock (the 7.10pm) had been held because of the line occupation at

An early afternoon view of Lydford Station looking towards the Southern Region side of the 'joint' signal box with 2-6-2T No. 5564 on its return journey to Plymouth, now hauling the 12.40pm ex-Launceston train. Note the snow beginning to build up over the rails (29.12.62).

S. P. Derek

After taking water at Tavistock South, No. 5564 (on the 12.40pm Launceston to Plymouth service) awaits the arrival of the 12.45pm train from Plymouth headed by 0–6–0PT No. 6400 (29.12.62).

Peter W. Gray

Opposite: The same train leaving Bickleigh Station in what had by then become extreme wintery conditions (29.12.62).

Peter W. Gray

Marsh Mills. As a result, once the other train had left the station confines, work began in earnest to clear and change the points again so that the Plymouth-bound train could at last leave. This, of course, had to be done manually in the most atrocious conditions imaginable. In fact, it was nearly midnight before the task was completed only for it then to be discovered that the 7.10pm train, with No. 6400 at its head, couldn't move – it was frozen to the rails! The outcome was that the footplate crew, after keeping up steam for as long as possible until a shortage of water meant dropping the fire, had to abandon the locomotive and join the signalman in his signal box for the night, along with the three remaining passengers – all 14 year-old lads.

Meanwhile, No. 5568 and its plucky crew, struggling to see the way ahead and under constant threat of a possible derailment due to the accumulations of drifting snow, pressed on through the night until eventually arriving at Tavistock South at 12.25am. Here, the dedication of the staff was admirable. It spite of having lost contact with the signalman at Lydford due to the telegraph wires having come down, they had made arrangements, by GPO telephone, to set up pilot working in order that the train could continue its journey: this was necessary because the rules stipulated that in such circumstances a driver had to have written authority from either the stationmaster or the signalman to enter their section. However, the pilotman (the stationmaster at Lydford) couldn't get through as the train on which he was to have travelled to Tavistock North (the 7.10pm Waterloo to Plymouth) was being held at Okehampton, unable to proceed because of snowdrifts blocking the line between Meldon and Lydford. Consequently, as with the 7.10pm Tavistock to Plymouth train at Bickleigh, the service had to be terminated.

0–6–0PT No. 6430 leaving Marsh Mills, and its snow-covered platforms, with the 2.10pm Plymouth to Tavistock South train (29.12.62).

Peter W. Gray

As usual, in such circumstances, help was soon at hand for the stranded passengers, and telephone messages being sent to their families, wherever possible. Some were content to spend the night aboard the train, whose driver kept up steam for as long as possible, while others were grateful to accept temporary overnight accommodation organised by members of the WVS and other voluntary organisations.

Sunday 30th December 1962

With morning light, arrangements for the rescue of the two marooned trains and their passengers were made. Help came to Bickleigh with No. 6430 and a recovery crew from Laira shed arriving on the scene – after a somewhat fraught journey taking some three hours! Armed with steam lances, they loosened the ice and snow on the trapped train and, at around 4pm, it was ready to be towed into Plymouth, complete with its three passengers and three others who had called at the station not realising that the line had, by then, been officially closed.

At Tavistock, meanwhile, those passengers and crew destined for Launceston were taken there by taxi. For the remainder, a special three-coach train was sent out from Plymouth, hauled by Bullied Pacific, No. 34063 *229 Squadron*. On reaching the outskirts of Tavistock North, however, it ground to a halt, unable to continue due to snow blocking the track and points. As a result, members of staff, assisted by passengers from the stranded 'last' train, set to work on clearing the way until, some two hours later, the train was able to pull into the station. With no hope of reaching train crews trapped by the blizzard at Lydford, No. 34063 then ran around its coaches, recoupled and set off on the return trip to Plymouth at 1.30pm.

The 7.10pm ex-Tavistock South train delayed at Bickleigh, with 0–6–0PT No. 6400 frozen to the rails and partly covered in snow and icicles (30.12.62).

R. E. Taylor

13

Three other scenes at Bickleigh on 30th December 1962:–

Top: A happy-looking, 6-year old Nigel Sharpe poses for the camera in front of the coaches of the stricken 7.10pm ex-Tavistock South train.

Centre: A steam lance, fed from 0–6–0PT No. 6430, being used to free pointwork by railway staff.

Bottom: 0–6–0PT No. 6430 coupled to No. 6400 and ready for the journey to Plymouth – the train now some 20 hours late!

R. E. Taylor

Monday 31st December 1962

The weather had relented and a thaw begun, so a relief engine and crew were sent out to Tavistock from Laira shed in order to clear and retrieve the 'last' train. Once released, No. 5568 and its ensemble then made its way back to Plymouth, at the same time becoming the last passenger train on the branch. The line that should have closed on the previous Saturday had finally 'died'.

A study of what is believed to be either No. 4591 or No. 5564 arriving at Bickleigh with the rescued No. 5568 and the Plymouth to Launceston train which had been stranded at Tavistock South (31.12.62).

R. E. Taylor

A farewell that came two days late! The commemorative headboard, which includes the initials of the companies to have previously owned the line, was made by the founder member of the Plymouth Railway Circle (the late Mr H. Liddle) and is depicted here on the bunker of 2–6–2T No. 5564 as it pauses at Marsh Mills with the 12.40pm Launceston to Plymouth train on 29th December 1962.

Eric R. Shepherd

15

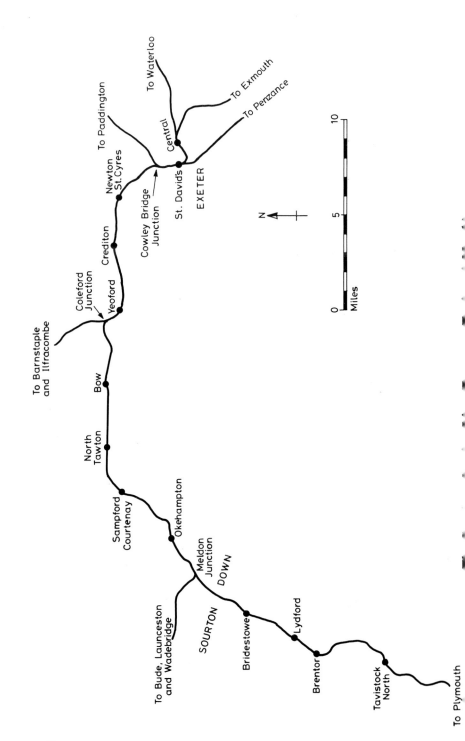

CHAPTER 2

The Battle on Sourton Down

One could be accused of overstatement by describing it as a battle, but it does best illustrate the events that unfolded, between 29th December 1962 and 21st February 1963, on the Southern Region main line between Okehampton and Tavistock – principally at Lydford and Sourton Down, both on the western edge of Dartmoor.

The weather did not usually create problems here; in fact, the line was more often than not used as a diversionary route when the sea wall was damaged by gales at Dawlish, on the Western Region main line between Exeter and Plymouth. But now, as in 1947, it was its turn to face the elements.

Saturday 29th December 1962

It began as a normal Saturday, with trains running on time, but in the afternoon the wind started causing trouble by blowing falling snow, as well as that already lying on the ground, into drifts. With daylight fading, Traffic Control at Exeter was becoming increasingly concerned by reports of the worsening conditions coming in from crews and staff on the moor, especially between Okehampton and Lydford, where the local permanent way gangs were seemingly fighting a losing battle to keep the lines clear.

An early afternoon view of Lydford Station looking towards the Western Region side of the 'joint' signal box as SR rebuilt Westcountry class Pacific 4–6–2 No. 34024 *Tamar Valley* arrives at the 'up' Southern Region platform on the 11.46am Plymouth to Waterloo service (29.12.62).

S. P. Derek

To make matters worse, the points were jamming at Meldon Junction and seriously affecting the North Cornwall line to Bude, Launceston and Wadebridge. As a result, it was decided to alert the snowplough crews at Exmouth Junction Locomotive Depot to be ready, at 9.30pm, to leave for the trouble spots.

The snowploughs, consisting of two 700 class 0–6–0 tender locomotives known as 'Black Motors', were of a design by Dugald Drummond. Now past their prime and already withdrawn from active service, they had been specifically retained for these duties, along with a third to act as standby. All were fitted with modern snowploughs designed to throw the snow clear of the tracks.

The two 700 class 0–6–0 tender locomotives, Nos. 30689 and 30697, photographed here at Exeter Central Station.

S. P. Derek

As was to be expected at a time when work on the railways was met with dedication and regarded more as a way of life than a mere job, the snowploughs left Exmouth Junction right on time, with Inspector Edgar Snow in charge. On the leading engine, Driver Yeo and his fireman were joined by Fitter John Watts and his mate, Peter Adams, who were assigned to work and adjust the ploughs. They, like their permanent way colleagues, were prepared for a long spell of duty.

Arriving at Okehampton, they were given the rather ominous news of a freight train having become stuck at Lydford. Nevertheless, armed with instructions and given permission to proceed, they subsequently left the relative shelter of the station to head into the blizzard which, by Meldon Quarry, was making its severity clear. Halting at the viaduct, John Watts left the footplate with a 'Tilly' oil lamp in order to check the track ahead and to ensure that snow wasn't blocking the check rails. This was to prove a difficult task in itself, for such was the force of the wind that the lamp was frequently blown horizontally.

After inching forward, they eventually reached the other side of the viaduct without incident and, with the fitter safely aboard once more, continued towards Meldon Junction. From here on ploughing began in earnest, the blades throwing the snow up into the air and clear of the track. Approaching Prewley summit, the drifts even needed a couple of charges, which meant reversing the engines and then going forward at full steam in order to clear them. The situation was deteriorating rapidly, and a house near the line at Sourton, acting as a windbreak, only aggravated the situation by causing the snow to pile up across the track. Needless to say, this slowed them considerably, and meant that it was close to midnight before Lydford was finally reached. Then disaster struck – the leading engine became derailed!

At this point, with the two locomotives quickly becoming engulfed by snow, it became obvious that no further work could be carried out. So, with fires banked up, the exhausted crews sought shelter at the nearby Lydford Hotel, joining the crew from the freight train already there. With only a few shillings between them, they then tried telephoning the District Superintendent at Exeter so that arrangements could be made to pay the bill for the unexpected board and lodgings, but such were the prevailing conditions that even that took several hours.

Sunday 30th December 1962

With the cold light of dawn, a surrealistic scene greeted the stranded train crews: the blizzard, now over, had left curiously-shaped contours where the rolling stock, buildings and other railway artefacts lay half-buried in the snow. In addition, the air was filled with an awesome silence, and the only sign of movement was smoke drifting lazily from the chimneys of the locomotives.

At Exeter, meanwhile, Traffic Control was busy putting into effect plans to clear the line and to free the trapped trains. In fact, another snowplough had already left Exmouth Junction Locomotive Depot before dawn and was now moving in from the Okehampton direction, its crew aided by railwaymen brought in from other areas as well as by troops from the 6th Training Battalion, R.A.S.C. Yeovil. Success, however, was to prove somewhat limited, for whilst they managed to clear a single-line path it was not wide enough for trains to pass through without running the risk of coaches fouling the wall of snow that had built up on either side of the line.

Later, a diesel snowplough, summoned from Laira with the aim of clearing the line from the other direction, passed through Tavistock North and continued towards Lydford. Unfortunately, though, it reached only as far as Mary Tavy before being in need of rescue itself – packed snow had caused its derailment! Furthermore, this meant that another train, carrying

Three photographs showing the surrealistic scene that greeted the stranded train crews at Lydford on the morning of 30th December 1962. The goods wagons are those of the trapped freight train that the snowploughs had hoped to retrieve.

J. Watts collection

troops from the Devon and Dorset Regiment, who had been assigned to help with the clearing-up operations, was unable to get through to the weary crews and troops at Lydford. And so, with water supplies frozen and the boilers getting low, the fires were dropped and the crews settled in at the hotel for another night.

Monday 31st December 1962

Early morning saw the temperature starting to rise sufficiently for a gentle thaw to set in, thus encouraging renewed efforts on the part of the workmen. But, in line with the weather forecast, the wind gradually strengthened and veered around to the east once more, and whilst they eventually succeeded in freeing one of the engines little other progress was made due to the return of the cold air.

Tuesday 1st January 1963

The New Year began with the workmen continuing in their efforts to reclaim the section of line between Tavistock and Lydford, which was still blocked, in places, by 12-feet high drifts. The task was made no easier by overnight freezing rain having glazed the snow, thus sealing in the cold and inhibiting any benefit from the rays of the sun. Nevertheless, by early afternoon the 'up' line had finally been cleared, the derailed diesel snowplough had been recovered and the trapped freight train freed to continue its journey eastwards as single line working was instituted. At the same time it was reported that on either side of the line the snow was piled as high as a house!

Throughout these developments the snowploughs at Lydford remained stuck on the 'down' line, but for the crews, who had by now spent some 48 hours away from home, relief had come at last.

Wednesday 2nd January 1963

By late morning the workmen, now almost totally exhausted, had also managed to clear the 'down' line, and the snowploughs at Lydford, both having been freed in the meantime, were subsequently towed back to Okehampton in order to thaw out prior to returning to base. Indeed, before long, train services were being re-instated, the passengers, no doubt, amazed by the sights that greeted them as they crossed the moor, with polar landscapes replacing the usual bracken and heather. They would also have seen the sad sight of moorland ponies and sheep scraping at the snow in search of food.

Thursday 3rd January 1963

At 8.45am snow began to fall again, and within a matter of hours a further five inches had been added to that already lying on the ground.

Roads became blocked and further problems arose on the railway, which resulted in trains being cancelled, including those between Brighton and Plymouth – in both directions.

In order to try and combat the blizzard conditions that soon prevailed once again, the snowploughs travelled the line on a regular basis, busily dispersing the snow blown across the tracks by the easterly wind. This proved to be quite effective, but for one of the drivers, on a trip from Tavistock to Lydford, it also brought about a heart-stopping moment. He passed a black object beside the line, pulled up and then reversed to the spot where it lay, thinking that it was a body. Much to his relief, however, he quickly discovered that it was nothing of the sort. Instead, it was merely a sheet of corrugated iron that had blown off some nearby moorland building!

Friday 4th January 1963 to Tuesday 8th January 1963

Throughout this period there was something of a respite, with temperatures rising above freezing point during the day and allowing a gradual thaw to set in. On the final day, though, it began to turn cold again, and more snow was forecast.

Wednesday 9th January 1963

After a morning of relative calm, the wind began to strengthen until, by early afternoon, another blizzard had developed. The snow, crystallized by the sub-zero temperatures into fine grains, then soon started to block the line again.

One of the first casualties on this occasion was 'N' class 2–6–0 No. 31838. This had been despatched from Exeter to assist a goods train stopped by the weather near Lydford, but by the time that Bridestowe had been reached it, too, had become overwhelmed. The crew, then faced with no choice other than to abandon the locomotive to the elements, went off to seek shelter in the nearest public house!

Coincidentally, the snowploughs were pressed into action whilst the storm was at its height and proceeded to engage in an already lost battle. This, in fact, was confirmed conclusively at Sourton cutting, where they became stuck in deepening drifts. Moreover, with the snow quickly rising to footplate level and invading the cabs of the locomotives, the crews could only emulate their colleagues at Bridestowe by abandoning their charges and seeking shelter. It was then, whilst in the process of doing this, and because of the vast accumulation of snow, that one of the men tripped – over the top of a signal! Meanwhile, because of the worsening conditions, the 11.30am Brighton to Plymouth train had already been re-routed via the Western Region main line from Exeter, as had the 9.00am and 11.00am ex-Waterloo services, the latter being the famed *Atlantic Coast Express*. Trains from Exeter and Plymouth, too, were soon being terminated at Okehampton and Lydford respectively.

Thursday 10th January 1963

The day after this latest blizzard saw around one hundred men trying to clear the line and release the trapped locomotives, but progress was severely hampered by sub-zero temperatures and a strong wind that persisted in blowing much of the snow back from where it was being removed. The huge drifts, well over 12 feet high in places, had to be cleared by hand due to no machinery being available, and although soldiers working at the Tavistock end of the main blockage tried blowing the snow clear with explosives this, too, achieved little in the way of success. All the while the men working at Sourton, their faces red because of the intense cold, and stinging from the snow-blowing around them, carried on shovelling as cheerfully as they could in such circumstances, hoping, eventually, to meet their fellow workers somewhere near the middle of the blockage. But, with the onset of darkness and falling temperatures, operations were brought to a halt, and it must have been heartbreaking for them to see what little had actually been achieved: the line was still blocked and only the goods train had been freed.

Friday 11th January 1963

A bitterly cold night, during which the temperature dropped to minus 8°C, was followed by the coldest day for 15 years. However, even with the temperature refusing to rise above minus 4°C, work continued unabated and ultimately resulted in the locomotive that had gone to assist the goods train two days earlier being released and towed back to Okehampton. The two snowplough engines, on the other hand, had still to be freed from the clutches of the huge drifts as daylight faded.

(At this point it is worth considering for a moment the hardships under which these men involved in the snow-clearance operations had to work, especially given the ambient temperatures and depth of the snow. Firstly, there was none of the modern-day, state-of-the-art equipment, just spades for shifting the snow. Secondly, protective clothing at that time was restricted, at best, to long woollen underwear, thick wool/cotton trousers and shirts, and woollen jumpers and jackets, or long sou'westers, the only exception being army-issue greatcoats, body warmers, footwear and hats for some of those who had served in the armed forces as conscripts. Most of them had to make do with wellingtons or hobnailed boots, and only a few wore gloves.)

Saturday 12 January 1963

After an even colder night, with Exeter Airport now also recording a low of minus 8°C, the moorland conditions were even more arctic-like when the workmen returned to concentrate on freeing the trapped snowploughs. BR, in the meantime, had been obliged to turn down further

Above and below: With a strong wind persisting in blowing snow across the track, tired workmen bend to the task of clearing the two snowplough engines trapped on Sourton Down (10.1.63).

Western Morning News (Courtesy of John Cheesman)

offers of help from the army in Plymouth, the reason being that the accumulation of snow, combined with the space occupied by the two locomotives, meant that there was simply insufficient room for more than a certain number of men to work.

Throughout the morning clear skies and a state of near calmness assisted progress considerably, and the workmen, spurred on by a determination to have the line opened by the end of the weekend, at last received some just reward for their efforts: after the track leading to the first of the snowploughs had been cleared, the locomotive itself was freed and subsequently removed to Okehampton.

Sunday 13th January 1963

Work now began in earnest to release the last engine, No. 30697, which, by this time, had been stuck in 12-feet drifts for no less than four days. Initially, once the snow had been shovelled away from the immediate vicinity, Fitter Reg Lang and his mate (Albert Davey), who had both travelled out from Exmouth Junction Locomotive Depot, lit fires of cotton waste soaked in paraffin under and against the frozen locomotive in an attempt to thaw out the bearings on wheels and coupling rods. After a while, though, Inspector Sam Smith (in charge of operations) decided to adopt rather more drastic measures in order to clear the line quickly: he stood back and signalled to Driver Jack Leathy and Fireman Peter King, now on the scene in a 'N' class 2–6–0, to shunt the frozen locomotive. At first this proved to be totally ineffective, apart from removing snow and icicles (some as long as 18 inches or more), and it was not until the sixth attempt that it was finally forced free of the rails to which it was frozen. Even at this point, however, its wheels still remained firmly locked, and it took yet another shunt – much heavier, and accompanied by a loud cracking noise – before No. 30697 was totally free.

Although it was obvious that the locomotive had sustained damage, Inspector Smith was delighted that the obstruction had finally been cleared and immediately made arrangements for it to be pushed slowly away to Okehampton – with a brake van placed between the two locomotives so as to even the load over Meldon viaduct for safety reasons. The workmen, meanwhile, soon knuckled down to the task of clearing the snow from the remaining 100 yards or so of track still covered by drifts, in readiness for the recommencement of normal traffic on the following morning.

Monday 14th January 1963

Contrary to expectations, the line remained closed to normal traffic due to an unforeseen problem at Sourton cutting – snow had collapsed from the sides of the cutting and blocked the track once more! As a result, the workmen had to be called out again and, in a temperature of minus 4°C, undertake the task of clearing what was estimated to be 200 wagon loads of snow before trains could get through.

Tuesday 15th January 1963 to Thursday 31st January 1963

Once the avalanches of snow had been cleared from Sourton cutting, the line was, at last, to enjoy a period of relative peace and calm from the elements. Nevertheless, the snowploughs (No. 30697 now having been replaced by two 'Q' class 0–6–0s, Nos. 30530 and 30531, which had been designed by R. E. L. Maunsell in 1936) were frequently in action throughout the rest of January, running up and down the section of track between Okehampton and Tavistock at a good speed so as to keep any fresh, or drifting, snow well clear. In order to keep travelling to a minimum for those concerned, the spare set of breakdown vans from Exmouth Junction Locomotive Depot was parked at Okehampton and a temporary base set up, the vans having accommodation and mess facilities.

The effect of ploughing at speed, incidentally, proved quite dramatic at times for, as described by Fitter John Watts, who travelled with the crews, "the snow thrown up into the air by the blades of the ploughs and then passing behind the locomotive, as it fell to the ground once more, created a 'tunnel' over those in the cab". John also recalls that on one particularly clear night the snow, being blown by an easterly wind, created a halo effect (complete with the colours of the rainbow) around the edge of the moon. On yet another occasion he saw a fox silhouetted by the moon, but this was a rather sad sight as the poor animal had frozen to death.

And so a very unusual January came to a close – but the battle was not yet completely over.

(Photographs depicting scenes along parts of the route between Okehampton and Tavistock on 16th January 1963 appear on the next four pages and are reproduced by kind permission of Mr S. P. Derek)

27

Below: Rebuilt Westcountry class Pacific 4-6-2 No. 34032 *Camelford* between Bridestowe and Lydford with the 9.00am Waterloo to Plymouth train.

Above: Rebuilt Westcountry class Pacific 4–6–2 No. 34036 *Westward Ho* near Lydford with the 11.46am Plymouth to Waterloo train.

Below: Rebuilt 'BB' class Pacific 4–6–2 No. 34060 *25 Squadron* near Lydford with the 11.55am Exeter Central to Plymouth train.

Opposite: 'BB' class 4–6–2 No. 34075 *264 Squadron* near Brentor with the 11.10am Plymouth to Brighton train.

CHAPTER 3

The Second Offensive

February began much the same as the preceding month with the weather closing in, bringing more snow. In fact, around six inches fell on Dartmoor and parts of the surrounding countryside during the first day, but it was not until the following Monday that there were signs of a repeat of the real problems, when the wind gathered strength and started blowing the snow into large drifts. The second phase of the battle was about to commence!

Tuesday 5th February 1963

Reported as the worst in living memory, the blizzard continued unabated with a force 9 gale causing enormous drifts of up to 20 feet deep in places and forcing the main line into closure once again. Among the trains affected on this occasion was the 11.46am Plymouth to Okehampton, which became stuck at Meldon Junction and resulted in two of its passengers seeking other means by which to complete their journeys. Another was the 3.48pm Exeter to Okehampton, stopped at Sampford Courtenay for four hours, along with its ten passengers, before being freed and able to continue, while the 3.13pm Bude to Okehampton train was held up at Ashbury. Others, too, were overwhelmed until, by the end of the day, no less than four locomotives, a passenger train and a freight train were stuck in, or under, drifts on the moor. To add to the problems, some of the passengers arriving at Exeter Central, bound for Plymouth via Okehampton, had to have emergency accommodation found for them in the city by BR staff.

Wednesday 6th February 1963

The line remained closed all day between Okehampton and Lydford, and resulted in many trains (including the 11.10am Plymouth to Brighton) having to be re-routed via the Western Region main line again, as in the previous month. Two locomotives lay buried in the snow near Meldon Quarry, a passenger train was stuck – now, for more than 24 hours – between Bridestowe and Lydford, and an assisting engine, as well as a snowplough, was similarly afflicted. In addition, on the freight side, Monday's 10.15pm Nine Elms (London) to Plymouth lay buried at Sourton, the scene of so many problems less than a month earlier.

With the battle engaged, twenty members of 29 Commando Regiment The Royal Artillery Plymouth joined a detachment of men from The Devon & Dorset Regiment in digging-out operations, while a further twenty men, from the Wessex Brigade depot at Honiton, provided assistance in trying to clear the line between Exeter and Okehampton.

Thursday 7th February 1963

The temperature now started to rise sufficiently for a gentle thaw to set in, but such were the vast accumulations of snow that the mammoth task of clearing the line went on all day and even into the night. One by one, though, the trapped locomotives and trains were freed, and the situation slowly began to return to normal once more.

Conclusion

Although further snow fell on the following Sunday, it was not accompanied by the harsh winds and low temperatures previously experienced with the result that it proved possible to keep the line clear and to maintain regular train services. This then remained the pattern until 21st February, when fresh blizzards developed and, at first, gave every indication of causing yet more trouble. On this occasion, however, there was to be a respite: the airflow changed to the south and, by the following morning, the snow – the last of the winter – had turned to rain.

Throughout the remainder of February the main concern was that of flooding due to the combined effects of further rain and the warmer air melting the snow that was left lying on the ground. Indeed, extensive flooding occurred in many places, but the railway line escaped largely unaffected save at Cowley Bridge Junction (the meeting point of the rivers Exe and Culm), where severe speed/load restrictions had to be imposed because the bridges had already been seriously weakened by floods in October of 1960 and were due to be replaced. Thereafter, with temperatures reaching 15°C, positively tropical compared with the previous months, the cold was soon forgotten as spring unfolded, and life on the line settled back into routine.

———————

CHAPTER 4

Other Lines

Prior to the winter of 1962/63 a number of other lines had penetrated parts of Dartmoor at one time or another, some dating back as far as the early 19th century. Most of them, by now having fallen into dis-use, had been constructed mainly for the movement of various products from the moor such as granite, peat, ores from the mines and china clay, but one of the few exceptions was the 12¼-mile line connecting Moretonhampstead with Newton Abbot, which carried passenger as well as freight trains.

Passenger services on this line, which had intermediate stations at Heathfield, Bovey and Lustleigh and three halts (Teigngrace (formerly a station), Brimley and Hawkmoor/Pullabrook), had ceased, however, in 1959. Consequently, apart from a freight service – usually once a day to serve a banana ripening factory and an oil depot at Heathfield, a malting plant at Bovey, and also to cater for clay traffic, supplies of domestic coal and other general goods – the line had fallen into dis-use with the result that the effect of the winter of 1962/63 caused no more than minimal disruption.

Another line often associated with this area, but barely touching the foothills of Dartmoor, was that running from Totnes to Ashburton. Here again, though, passenger services had already ceased (in 1958) and, moreover, the line had been closed to all traffic on and from 10th September 1962 – just over three months before the events described in this book unfolded!

CHAPTER 5

Postscript

The cost of the attempts to keep the Southern Region main line clear between Exeter and Tavistock, and between Okehampton and Lydford, in particular, was enormous, running into millions of pounds. That winter, with its accompanying severity of temperature, wind and snow, has yet to be repeated and even if (or when) such weather should return, Dartmoor would no longer resound to the pounding of steam engines fighting their way through blizzards and snowdrifts. Neither would poorly-dressed men, cigarette in mouth, be seen battling against the elements, determined in their efforts to keep the line open, for, by the end of the decade, all passenger services had been withdrawn and the track lifted beyond Meldon.

Of the three snowploughs initially brought into service from Exmouth Junction Locomotive Depot, No. 30697 had been declared a write-off following an inspection carried out at Okehampton shed. In the shunting operations to free the class 700 locomotive from Sourton cutting, one of its pistons, in trying to compress ice that had formed in the cylinder from condensed steam, had stopped and caused the cylinder cover to give way, taking with it part of the cylinder and effectively terminating the engine's life. As a result, in March 1963, with the damaged parts removed and its motion cut through for safety reasons, it was taken on its final journey to the scrapyard. By that time the two 'Q' class 0–6–0s (Nos. 30530 and 30531), brought in to replace it, had also departed from the area, both having returned to their home depot earlier that same month.

The two remaining class 700 locomotives, Nos. 30700 and 30689, on the other hand, completed their winter duties before returning to Exeter under their own steam and being left to rest (and rust) at the rear of St. David's locomotive shed until January 1964. They were then steamed and went on to complete their final journeys to the scrapyard, subsequently being replaced by two ex-GWR 0–6–0s, Nos. 2214 and 2277 (fitted with older-style, GWR wedge ploughs). However, neither of these replacements was destined to remain at Exeter for any length of time: by May of that same year No. 2277 had, itself, been replaced by another locomotive of the same class (No. 3205), while No. 2214 was removed during the following winter. Much the same was also to apply to No. 3205, which was withdrawn from service shortly after working a 'special' in the spring of 1965 – prior to departing for Totnes (and preservation) during the summer behind 2–6–2T No. 4555, on another 'special' that had arrived at Exeter earlier in the day behind No. 4079 *Pendennis Castle*.

With steam at this time rapidly disappearing and becoming no more than a memory, the locomotive depot at Exmouth Junction (once the largest in the South West) was, initially, relegated to a fuelling point and light maintenance depot. But then, on 6th March 1967, it was closed and the work transferred to Newton Abbot and to Exeter St. David's fuelling point. So, in the space of just a few years, things changed completely.

BIBLIOGRAPHY

British Weather Disasters, Ingrid Holford (David & Charles, 1976)

Express and Echo (30th December 1962 to 28th February 1963)

The Branch, Bernard Mills (Plym Valley Railway, 1983)

The Heathfield to Exeter (Teign Valley) Railway, Lawrence W. Pomroy (ARK Publications (Railways), 1995)

The Moretonhampstead and South Devon Railway, S. C. Jenkins and L. J. Pomroy (The Oakwood Press, 1989)

The Plymouth Tavistock and Launceston Railway, Anthony R. Kingdom (ARK Publications, 1990)

The Tavistock, Launceston & Princetown Railways, G. H. Anthony, M.C.I.T. (The Oakwood Press, 1971)

The Totnes to Ashburton Railway (and The Totnes Quay Line), Anthony R. Kingdom (ARK Publications (Railways), 1995)

The Withered Arm, T. W. E. Roche (Forge Books, 1984)

Western Morning News (30th December 1962 to 28th February 1963)